ENCOURAGEMENT

ENCOURAGEMENT

Ariel Books

Andrews and McMeel
Kansas City

Frontispiece: Claude Monet, *The Artist's Garden, Irises* 1900

All paintings by Claude Monet

Book design by Diane Stevenson of Snap-Haus Graphics

ISBN: 0-8362-4743-4

INTRODUCTION

$\mathcal{E}$veryone needs encouragement from time to time. It can come in the form of a hand stretched out in friendship, a vote of confidence when we need it most, a reassuring word, or a heartening smile. All of these are things that can lift our spirits and remind us of our own potential. Each person has a unique ability to grow, change, and deal with whatever comes along, be it an opportunity to be seized, an obstacle to be overcome, or a problem to be solved. Not all motivation and reassurance comes to us from others—much of it can be found within ourselves, through contemplation and self-awareness.

Whether encouragement comes from within or from other sources, what becomes clear is the same—we are worthy of the good that comes our way and can surmount and transcend the obstacles we encounter. This book will provide food for thought, which may lead to self-awareness and the exciting and invigorating discovery of our inner reserves—of faith, energy, and an unlimited capacity for growth.

First say to yourself what you would be; and then do what you have to do.

—EPICTETUS

Life is what we make it, always has been, always will be.

—GRANDMA MOSES

Every calling is great when greatly pursued.

—OLIVER WENDELL HOLMES, JR.

The person who makes a success of living is the one who sees his goal steadily and aims for it unswervingly. That is dedication.

—CECIL B. DEMILLE

Don't be afraid to take a big step if one is indicated. You can't cross a chasm in two small jumps.

—DAVID LLOYD GEORGE

The rung of a ladder was never meant to rest upon, but only to hold a man's foot long enough to enable him to put the other somewhat higher.

—THOMAS HENRY HUXLEY

You may be disappointed if you fail, but you are doomed if you don't try.

—BEVERLY SILLS

A journey of a thousand miles must begin with a single step.

—LAO-TZU

Life is a great big canvas; throw all the paint on it you can.

—DANNY KAYE

Not to go back is somewhat to advance.

—HORACE

*L*ife is a succession of moments. To live each one is to succeed.

—CORITA KENT

*Y*ou can do what you have to do, and sometimes you can do it even better than you think you can.

—JIMMY CARTER

*J*ust don't give up trying to do what you really want to do. Where there's love and inspiration, I don't think you can go wrong.

—ELLA FITZGERALD

I pray hard, work hard, and leave the rest to God.

—FLORENCE GRIFFITH JOYNER

*R*emember, you can't steal second if you don't take your foot off first.

—MIKE TODD

God helps those who persevere.
—The Koran, VIII

Success is never a destination—it's a journey.
—Satenig St. Marie

Keep making the movements of life.
—Thornton Wilder

Creativity is inventing, experimenting, growing, taking risks, breaking rules, making mistakes, and having fun.
—Mary Lou Cook

He has half the deed done who has made a beginning.
—Horace

You've got to take the initiative and play your game . . . confidence makes the difference.

—CHRIS EVERT

Never look down to test the ground before taking your next step; only he who keeps his eye fixed on the far horizon will find his right road.

—DAG HAMMARSKJÖLD

Hope in every sphere of life is a privilege that attaches to action. No action, no hope.

—PETER LEVI

Attempt the impossible in order to improve your work.

—BETTE DAVIS

The story is told of a king who issued a challenge to his wise men. He demanded they produce something so that when he felt despair and looked at it, the object would offer him hope, and that when he felt joy and looked at it, the object would remind him of his mortality. The thinkers gave their king a ring on which was inscribed this saying: "This too shall pass."

Let us follow our destiny, ebb and flow. Whatever may happen, we master fortune by accepting it.

—VIRGIL

Although the world is full of suffering, it is full also of the overcoming of it.

—HELEN KELLER

Keep your faith in all beautiful things; in the sun when it is hidden, in the Spring when it is gone.

—ROY R. GILSON

Great works are performed not by strength but by perseverance.

—SAMUEL JOHNSON

If a man does not keep pace with his companions, perhaps it is because he hears a different drummer. Let him step to the music which he hears, however measured or far away.

—HENRY DAVID THOREAU

Our greatest glory is not in never falling but in rising every time we fall.

—Confucius

You have to accept whatever comes and the only important thing is that you meet it with courage and with the best that you have to give.

—Eleanor Roosevelt

You commit a sin of omission if you do not utilize all the power that is within you.

—Oliver Wendell Holmes

Ah, but a man's reach should exceed his grasp, Or what's a heaven for?

—Robert Browning

I know of no more encouraging fact than the unquestionable ability of man to elevate his life by a conscious endeavor.

—Henry David Thoreau

The only way to meet affliction is to pass through it solemnly, slowly, with humility and faith, as the Israelites passed through the sea. Then its very waves of misery will divide, and become to us a wall, on the right side and on the left, until the gulf narrows before our eyes, and we land safe on the opposite shore.

—DINAH MARIA MULOCK

Life is either a daring adventure or nothing at all. Security is mostly a superstition. It does not exist in nature.

—HELEN KELLER

It is necessary to try to pass one's self always; this occupation ought to last as long as life.

—QUEEN CHRISTINA OF SWEDEN

They can do all because they think they can.

—VIRGIL

Most people are familiar with the feeling of suppressing anger, when we're afraid to let out negative feelings. But we can also suppress happiness. Every emotion we experience should have its place in our lives. We should acknowledge our feelings, live through them, and experience what they mean for us. We must allow ourselves the luxury of our own emotions—express, don't suppress!

*B*e strong and of good courage; be not afraid, neither be thou dismayed: for the Lord thy God is with thee whithersoever thou goest.

—Joshua 1:9

*T*here is a budding morrow in midnight.

—John Keats

*O*pen your eyes! The world is still intact; it is as pristine as it was on the first day, as fresh as milk!

—Paul Claudel

*W*hen you get into a tight place and everything goes against you, till it seems as though you could not hang on a minute longer, never give up then, for that is just the place and time that the tide will turn.

—Harriet Beecher Stowe

Ride on! Rough-shod if need be, smooth-shod if that will do, but ride on! Ride on over all obstacles, and win the race!

—CHARLES DICKENS

Life is not easy for any of us. But what of that? We must have perseverance and above all confidence in ourselves. We must believe that we are gifted for something, and that this thing, at whatever cost, must be attained.

—MARIE CURIE

I am not afraid of storms for I am learning how to sail my ship.

—LOUISA MAY ALCOTT

I will spit on my hands and take better hold.

—JOHN HEYWOOD

ever mention the worst. Never think of it. Drop it out of your consciousness. At least ten times every day affirm, "I expect the best and with God's help will attain the best." In so doing your thoughts will turn toward the best and become conditioned to its realization. This practice will bring all of your powers to focus on the attainment of the best. It will bring the best to you.

—NORMAN VINCENT PEALE

*Y*ou have to believe in happiness or happiness never comes.

—Douglas Malloch

*P*eople who pray for miracles usually don't get miracles. . . . But people who pray for courage, for strength to bear the unbearable, for the grace to remember what they have left instead of what they have lost, very often find their prayers answered. . . . Their prayers helped them tap hidden reserves of faith and courage which were not available to them before.

—Harold S. Kushner

I could not, at any age, be content to take my place in a corner by the fireside and simply look on. Life was meant to be lived. Curiosity must be kept alive. The fatal thing is the rejection. One must never, for whatever reason, turn his back on life.

—Eleanor Roosevelt

wo monks were walking along and came to a shallow but rapidly flowing river. A young woman, obviously unable to get across, stood helplessly at the water's edge. The older monk offered to carry her across. She accepted, and he deposited her safely on the other side. The monks then continued on their journey. After about a mile, the younger monk said, "How could you have done that? It's against our orders to have any contact with women." The older monk replied, "Are you still carrying her? I left her at the river."

—Zen story

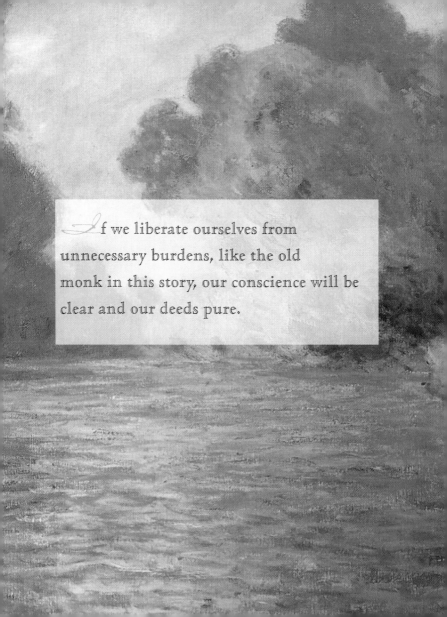

If we liberate ourselves from unnecessary burdens, like the old monk in this story, our conscience will be clear and our deeds pure.

*I*f you want to be respected by others the great thing is to respect yourself. Only by that, only by self-respect will you compel others to respect you.

—FYODOR DOSTOEVSKY

*T*he English word "crisis" is translated by the Chinese with two little characters; one means "danger," the other "opportunity."

—JEAN HOUGK

*J*ust trust yourself, then you will know how to live.

—JOHANN WOLFGANG VON GOETHE

*Y*ou have to accept whatever comes and the only important thing is that you meet it with the best you have to give.

—ELEANOR ROOSEVELT

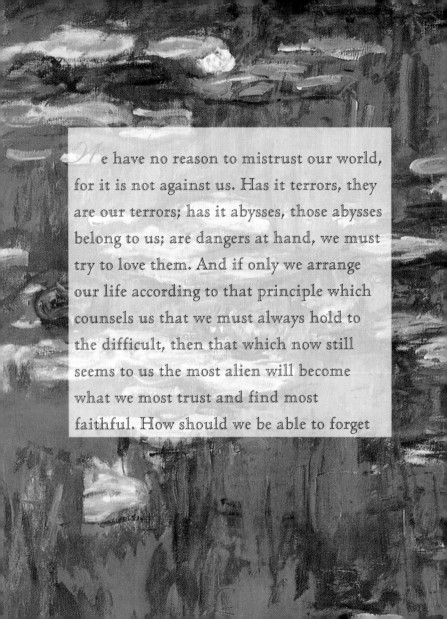

e have no reason to mistrust our world,
for it is not against us. Has it terrors, they
are our terrors; has it abysses, those abysses
belong to us; are dangers at hand, we must
try to love them. And if only we arrange
our life according to that principle which
counsels us that we must always hold to
the difficult, then that which now still
seems to us the most alien will become
what we most trust and find most
faithful. How should we be able to forget

those ancient myths that are at the beginning of all peoples, the myths about dragons that at the last moment turn into princesses; perhaps all the dragons of our lives are princesses who are only waiting to see us once beautiful and brave. Perhaps everything terrible is in its deepest being something helpless that wants help from us.

—Rainer Maria Rilke,
LETTERS TO A YOUNG POET

*P*lunge boldly into the thick of life!
—Johann Wolfgang von Goethe

*L*ook, I really don't want to wax philosophic, but I will say that if you're alive, you got to flap your arms and legs, you got to jump around a lot, you got to make a lot of noise, because life is the very opposite of death. And therefore, as I see it, if you're quiet, you're not living . . . you've got to be noisy, or at least your *thoughts* should be noisy and colorful and lively.

—Mel Brooks

*N*othing in life is to be feared. It is only to be understood.

— MARIE CURIE

*B*e not afraid of life. Believe that life *is* worth living, and your belief will help create the fact.

— WILLIAM JAMES

*M*ake voyages! Attempt them . . . there's nothing else.

— TENNESSEE WILLIAMS

One of the things I learned the hard way was that it doesn't pay to get discouraged. Keeping busy and making optimism a way of life can restore your faith in yourself.

—Lucille Ball

Every thing that is done in the world is done by hope.

—Martin Luther

No single event can awaken within us a stranger totally unknown to us. To live is to be slowly born.

—Antoine de Saint-Exupéry

The idea of being born slowly as we live and learn is one worth considering. We are always changing, adapting, and growing— while remaining true to our inner selves at the same time.

We should take the time to learn who we have become and celebrate the advances we have made, reflecting on where we have been and looking forward with anticipation to where we want to go.

ENCOURAGEMENT

ENCOURAGEMENT

To travel hopefully is better than to arrive.

—SIR JAMES JEANS

No matter how dark things seem to be or actually are, raise your sights and see the possibilities—always see them, for they're always there.

—NORMAN VINCENT PEALE

To live is so startling it leaves little time for anything else.

—EMILY DICKINSON

Change your life today. Don't gamble on the future, act now, without delay.

—SIMONE DE BEAUVOIR

All growth is a leap in the dark, a spontaneous, unpremeditated act without benefit of experience.

—HENRY MILLER

single gentle rain makes the grass many shades greener. So our prospects brighten on the influx of better thoughts. We should be blessed if we lived in the present always, and took advantage of every accident that befell us, like the grass which confesses the influence of the slightest dew that falls on it; and did not spend our time in atoning the neglect of past opportunities, which we call doing our duty. We loiter in winter while it is already spring.

—Henry David Thoreau,
WALDEN

Keep love in your heart. . . . The consciousness of loving and being loved brings a warmth and
richness to life that nothing else can bring.

—Oscar Wilde

If winter comes, can spring be far behind?

—Percy Bysshe Shelley

In the depth of winter, I finally learned that
within me there lay an invincible summer.

—Albert Camus

Love many things, for therein lies the true strength,
and whosoever loves much performs much, and can
accomplish much, and what is done in love is well
done.

—Vincent van Gogh

There is only one real failure possible; and that is,
not to be true to the best one knows.

—Canon Farrar

When we do the best that we can, we never know what miracle is wrought in our life, or in the life of another.

—HELEN KELLER

Talk happiness. The world is sad enough
Without your woe. No path is wholly rough.

—ELLA WHEELER WILCOX

The essence of optimism is that it takes no account of the present, but it is a source of inspiration, of vitality and hope where others have resigned; it enables a man to hold his head high, to claim the future for himself and not to abandon it to his enemy.

—DIETRICH BONHOEFFER

So of cheerfulness, or a good temper, the more it is spent, the more of it remains.

—RALPH WALDO EMERSON

One only gets to the top rung on the ladder by steadily climbing up one at a time, and suddenly all sorts of powers, all sorts of abilities which you thought *never* belonged to you—suddenly become within your own possibility and you think, well, I'll have a go, too.

—MARGARET THATCHER

Life appears to me too short to be spent in nursing animosity or registering wrong.

—CHARLOTTE BRONTË

Life shrinks or expands in proportion to one's courage.

—ANAÏS NIN

It seems to me we can never give up longing and wishing while we are alive. There are certain things we feel to be beautiful and good, and we must hunger for them.

—GEORGE ELIOT

*H*e knows not his own strength that hath not met adversity.

— BEN JONSON

*B*elieve there is a great power silently working all things for good, behave yourself and never mind the rest.

— BEATRIX POTTER

*W*e should not let our fears hold us back from pursuing our hopes.

— JOHN F. KENNEDY

*I*t's too bad that one has to conceive of sports as being the only arena where risks are, [for] all of life is risk exercise. That's the only way to live more freely, and more interestingly.

— WILLIAM SLOANE COFFIN, JR.

ENCOURAGEMENT

ENCOURAGEMENT

Nothing is too small to know, and nothing too big to attempt.

—WILLIAM VAN HORNE

The year's at the spring
And day's at the morn;
Morning's at seven;
The hillside's dew-pearled;
The lark's on the wing;
The snail's on the thorn:
God's in his heaven—
All's right with the world.

—ROBERT BROWNING

You need only claim the events of your life to make yourself yours. When you truly possess all you have been and done, which may take some time, you are fierce with reality.

—FLORIDA SCOTT-MAXWELL